The Grand Betrayal
of Western Christianity

The Grand Betrayal
of Western Christianity

James M. Houston

REGENT COLLEGE PUBLISHING
Vancouver, British Columbia

Dedicated to my great-grandchildren, as they face all the challenges of the Dark Age ahead.

The Grand Betrayal of Western Christianity
Copyright © 2021 James M. Houston

Regent College Publishing
5800 University Boulevard
Vancouver, BC V6T 2E4 Canada

All rights reserved. No part of this publication may be reproduced, stored in a retrieval system, or transmitted, in any form or by any means, electronic, mechanical, photocopying, recording or otherwise, without the prior written permission of the author, except in the case of brief quotations embodied in critical articles and reviews.

Regent College Publishing is an imprint of the Regent Bookstore (RegentBookstore.com). Views expressed in works published by Regent College Publishing are those of the author and do not necessarily represent the official position of Regent College (Regent-College.edu).

ISBN: 978-1-57383-597-8

Contents

1. The Anatomy of Betrayal • 1
2. The Betrayal of Early Christian Music • 9
3. Ecclesial Betrayals of the Middle Ages • 15
4. The Betrayals of the Reformation • 23
5. Deism as the Betrayal of Christian Faith • 33
6. The Betrayal of Christian Emotions • 39
7. The Modern Betrayal of Capitalism • 47
8. The Betrayal of Christian Aesthetics • 55
9. The Moral Betrayal of Our Major Institutions • 63
10. Challenging a "Fluid Culture" • 79
11. Christian Faithfulness to the Gospel of Christ • 95

Appendix: Responding to Being a Christian • 107

The Anatomy of Betrayal

> To prove my definition of secularism (i.e. "negation of worship") is correct I must prove two points. One concerning worship: it must be proven that the very notion of worship implies a certain idea of man's relationship not only to God, but also to the world. And one concerning secularism: it must be proven precisely that it is exactly this idea of worship that secularism explicitly or implicitly rejects.
> —Alexander Schmemann[1]

For the Christian, the narrative of betrayal begins with the event of the Last Supper in the Upper Room that Jesus shared with his disciples, where he said, "One of you will betray me." Appropriately it is Matthew, the former tax collector, that retells the story, as he had been a tax collector, a "quisling" to his fellow Jews. Now as a repentant disciple of Jesus, he narrates the dastardly event.

---

1. Alexander Schmemann, *For the Life of the World: Sacraments and Orthodoxy* (Crestwood, NY: St. Vladimir's Seminary Press, 1998), 119.

Knowing about betrayal, Matthew records that the disciples were very sad, each responding, "Surely you don't mean me, Lord?" (Matt. 26: 21-22). Then Judas, the one who would betray him, also asked, "Surely, you don't mean me, Rabbi?" (v. 25). No doubt, Judas, from the beginning, had simmered at the thought of Jesus calling a tax collector, when he himself was a Zealot, proud of being a defender of Israel. In all probability, Judas turned against Jesus because he judged that Jesus was betraying the Zealots' political cause.

This narrative, set in a distant time, is no different from the inner narrative of our emotions today. Every time I take the bread and wine at the Lord's table, I ask myself, "Is it I who this past week has denied the Lord?" For on one occasion I was silent in conversation when secularists were scorning Christianity. My silence was a denial that I was one of the Lord's disciples. I have daily then to recite the Lord's Prayer: "Forgive us our trespasses." Yet I continue to deny my Lord so frequently that it can become a way of life. Now at the end of my life, it is this question, "Is it I Lord?" that is challenging me to write this book.

The Anatomy of Denial

No doubt a lack of loyalty begins in our childhood. Perhaps basic trust was impaired as a small child when I could not trust one or both of my parents. Perhaps I have struggled to believe in God, especially if I have had many unanswered prayers for my deepest needs. The "Bible belt culture" has become hugely disenchanted with God for this same reason. "God answers prayer" we have chanted, but has he really done so, when his silence has been so dense? And our prayers for loved ones have gone unanswered!

Distrust leads to betrayal. It starts with the erosion or absence of basic trust. It may come from an absentee father, an angry mother, or a frightened parent who struggles with deep weaknesses. Fear then is generated in the child, and he or she grows up in an environment of secrecy. Like sex, secrecy can be intoxicating, and so the child grows up as the Russian novelist Chekhov narrates: "He had two lives: one open, seen and known by all who cared to know . . . and the other running its course in secret."

A split then occurs in one's identity, ranging from mild to extreme, as in psychotic patients. Fear dominates rather than love. Fear of authority then becomes instinctive and the act of disobedience ingrained. Just as a mother may conceal her truer feelings from her husband, so siblings may also keep their secrets from each other. Then instead of the nurture of basic trust, in a fragmented family secrecy may be the alternative bonding for all. Indeed, secrecy may become an alternative religion far more powerful than being a Christian!

We can all so easily develop two different personalities, as Ben Macintyre re-depicts in the narrative of a Soviet double agent who had two different personalities. Four lines from Kipling are apt:

> Something I owe to the soil that grew,
> More to the life that fed.
> But most to Allah who gave me two
> Separate sides to my head.[2]

Kim Philby, the British double agent, could inspire and convey affection with such ease that few noticed they were being charmed. According to a friend, "You didn't just like him, admire him, agree with him; you worshipped him."[3] Philby lived under the shadow of an imposing father, whose approval Philby longed to have and never quite received. He was brought up by nannies and then was sent to a distant boarding school.[4] As a young spy, alcohol helped to blunt the stress of clandestine war, as both a lubricant and a new bond with his friends. He had two lives: one open, seen and known by all who cared, and the other, running its course in secrecy.

---

2. Ben Macintyre, *A Spy Among Friends* (London: Penguin/Random House, 2014), 35.
3. Macintyre, *A Spy Among Friends*, 19.
4. Macintyre, *A Spy Among Friends*, 27-28.

Like Kilby, the Soviet double agent Oleg Gordievsky, was shaped in a similar way, with a frightened father who gave him no support. He grew up in a secretive household where even his brothers did not share their inner lives with each other. While stationed in Denmark in the 1960s, Gordievsky became enamored with a Western culture that was more open. Disillusioned, especially after the crushing of the Prague Spring in 1968, Gordievsky "crossed over" becoming an informer for the British. Eventually, after being extracted from Russia, and settling in Britain with his reunited family, his marriage "swiftly disintegrated." Today he lives in secrecy, alone, and under an assumed identity.[5]

Fear is our basic human emotion whereas love is its antithesis. The aged apostle John affirms this when he writes: "Perfect love drives out all fear" (1 John 4:18). Hence, we can say that sin is anti-relational and that Satan, as the anti-Christ, is the cosmic being that is incapable of love. Hell then is the sphere where one is incapable of loving or of being loved. This is why it is highly counterproductive for "Bible belt" Christians to threaten their rebellious teenagers, telling them that they are going to hell if they don't believe in God. As the apostle adds: "Everyone who believes that Jesus is

---

5. Ben Macintyre, *The Spy and the Traitor* (London: Viking, 2018) 8-11, 329-30.

the Son of God is born of God, and everyone who loves the Father loves his child as well" (1 John 5:1).

As educators well know, the formation of basic trust in a small child is formative of the growth of the later personality. It is basic for a Christian, and equally basic for a traitor. It shaped the disciple John as it shaped Judas. It shapes or disforms all of us.

Our Public Selves

But we are also shaped by culture and societal changes. These occur gradually, almost imperceptibly, although now speeding up much faster. It is best expressed in the nursery rhyme:

> For the loss of the nail, the shoe was lost.
> For the loss of the shoe, the horse was lost.
> For the loss of the horse, the rider was lost.
> For the loss of the rider, the battle was lost.
> For the loss of the battle, the kingdom was lost.
> All for the loss of the horseshoe nail!

This is a much more accurate interpretation of our secular culture than the idea of "an atheist revolution" of these past two decades. Yet this is the claim of the discussions transcribed by Stephen Fry in *The Four Horsemen: The Conversation That Sparked an Atheist Revolution*.[6] In this transcribed conversation, it is

6. Stephen Fry, *The Four Horsemen: The Conversation That Sparked an Atheist Revolution* (London: Bantam, 2019.

first expressed by Richard Dawkins, when he speaks of "the hubris of religion, the humility of science, and its intellectual and moral courage." Dawkins has demonstrated remarkable psychical courage in his pursuit of a brilliant career in biology. But the moral abstractions that he and his three colleagues postulate do not exist, since morals can only apply to personal human beings. So their generalizations are bad history, poor sociology, and failed philosophy. Yet, ironically, they cannot get away from the biblical influence of our Christian cultural heritage in titling their book The Four Horsemen, that is, "the four horsemen of the apocalypse" referred to in the book of Revelation.

But their polemical approach to attacking Christianity also helps us avoid a misguided riposte against secularism as an ideology. It is far more rooted in our history and therefore far more widespread in our culture today and cannot be countered by arguing ideologically or even just logically in a vigorous public debate. Such mental entertainment scarcely scratches the surface of such attitudes of unbelief. That is why this book takes a wholly different approach to understanding the major changes in Western civilization. It requires of us to harness all the major disciplines of contemporary scholarship in order to at least sketch out the profile of secularism today. This small contribution is only made possible because of my early professional training as an historian of ideas, combined with the privilege of knowing personally some of the wise and significant Christian leaders of our time. Now at the end of my life, approaching being a centenarian, I have lived to witness major cultural changes.

My motive for writing this book is to encourage a new generation that may feel like David; a small youth facing the giant Goliath. Be not afraid! The Lord is with those that put their trust in Him.

> You brought me out of the womb;
> You made me trust in you,
> Even at my mother's breast.
> From birth I was cast on you;
> From my mother's womb,
> You have been my God! (Ps. 22: 9-10)

2

The Betrayal of Early Christian Music

Early man learned two forms of communication: music and words. It appears that Neanderthal man first communicated by means of a primitive flute made from the wing of a small bird. When facing giant beasts like the mammoth on melting ice sheets across Eurasia, they learned to collaborate and mutually support each other. Homo sapiens evolved in the Rift Valley of the Upper Nile and could hunt small beasts at water holes in solitary fashion without communal co-operation. Their language, used more competitively within very small communities, evolved. The novelist William Golding highlighted this contrast in his novel *The Inheritors*.

Much later, worship as embodied in the Psalms, some traceable to the Iron Age, used melody in worship and also therapeutically, as we see in a young David playing to soothe the fears of King Saul. Even later the Greeks developed the theme of cosmic harmony, that is, "the music of the spheres," which was developed in a profound way in the Psalms. Praise to the creator requires the whole cosmos to be his temple, a theme many of the psalms celebrate. Indeed the mountains, the seas, and all creation praise him.

Much later the theme of the cosmic harmony of the psalms was interpreted by the early church as expressive of the eternal, immutable truths that unify and harmonize every part of reality into three realms: the macrocosm of the stars and spheres and the microcosm of the human soul, all expressed in the playing of simple musical instruments.

The church fathers memorized the words of the Psalms and sang them daily. By the fourth century Jerome reports that they were sung by women spinning their wool, by fishermen casting their nets, and by farmers ploughing their fields. While the fathers were vehement in their rejection of some of the music in the pagan society around them and did not allow it within their households and house churches, according to C. Harrison, "they balanced that negativity with a nearly unanimous enthusiastic affirmation of another kind of music . . . notably the Psalms, and in particular their hearing and chanting could enchant the soul, unifying, harmonizing, and ordering it, so that it converted towards, participated in, and resonated with the cosmic harmony of the Creator."[1] The church fathers

1. C. Harrison, "Enchanting the Heart: The Music of the Psalms," in *Meditations of the Heart: The Psalms in Early Christian*

vehemently rejected the introduction of pagan songs into Christian households and house churches.[2] They employed the cosmology of music to affect the "microcosm of the soul."[3] As Hans Boersma has stated, Clement of Alexander appropriates "the Platonic approach that linked cosmic harmony, the harmony of the soul, and the harmony of music."[4]

But as Christianity grew more prominent in Roman society, so too compromise with pagan music increased. John Chrysostom (c. 347-407) spoke boldly against Christian compromise with Roman culture, including music. Writing from Syria, he denounced the presence of pagan music at Christian weddings with its "dancing and cymbals, and flutes, and shameful words, and songs, and revellings, and all the Devil's great heap

---

Thought and Practice: Essays in Honour of Andrew Louth, ed. A. Andreopoulos, A. Casiday, and C. Harrison (Turnhout : Brepols, 2011), chap. 11.

2. C. Harrison, "Enchanting the Heart."

3. C. R. Stapert, *A New Song for an Old World: Musical Thought in the Early Church* (Grand Rapids: Eerdmans, 2007), 207. But see Clement of Alexandria's work, Exhortations to the Heathen, where he ironically quotes mythical accounts of how Amphion removed mountains with his lyre, Arion tamed dolphins with his singing, and Orpheus commanded all of nature by his singing. Then he adds, "Yes, and Eunomos transformed music with the chirp of the grasshopper!" (50-54).

4. H. Boersma, *Scripture as Real Presence: Sacramental Exegesis* (Grand Rapids: Baker, 2017), 149.

of garbage."[5] As he writes in his commentary on 1 Corinthians, he is reminded that the apostle Paul has already rebuked the early church there of similar abuses. Athanasius (c. 296-373), in his Letter to Marcellinus, had already warned his readers that the power of the Psalms did not come from its aesthetics. He writes: "[T]he Psalms were "to be chanted with melodies and strains. For some of the simple among us, although they believe that the phrases are divinely inspired, imagine however, on account of the sweetness of sound, that also the psalms are rendered musically for the sake of the ear's delight. But this is not so."[6]

Augustine of Hippo (354-430) from early in his conversion took music seriously. One of his early works is *De Musica* (c. 387). In it Augustine noted that sound has points of similarity with grammar and should be a serious study in itself. He developed various terms to express this "language of the soul." Music, he argued, was the language of the connections of emotions, stimulating desires of the heart for beauty, desirability, and attraction. Music is delectable, hence memorable. This is what modern neuroscience has discovered with Alzheimer's patients, that music is deeply developed in the brain. In *De Musica*, Augustine asks: "Where is

5. Quoted by Stapert, *A New Song for an Old World*, 122.
6. Athanasius, *The Life of Anthony and the Letter to Marcellinus*, trans. R. C. Gregg (Mahwah, NJ: Paulist Press, 1979), 121.

music?" His answer is that music is in sound in the ears, in the heart, our innermost recesses, in the mind, in the memory, and in terms of numbers sounded and remembered. Music possesses both a bodily and a spiritual reality. Then, following the Greeks, Augustine saw "the music of the spheres" as expressing cosmic harmony between the soul of man as the microcosm, and with the macrocosm of the whole universe.[7]

It is regrettable that the generations following Augustine forgot this Treatise, *De Musica*, in what we might call a "slow betrayal." Likewise, it is regrettable that the memorization of the Psalter became a lost practice; it was no longer an educational manual within Roman Christianity. But overseas, in the Celtic church of Ireland, it lingered. For in peat bogs, archaeologists have discovered slates used to teach children their lessons by singing the psalms in melody. This probably continued until the seventh and eighth centuries. As we shall see later, the memorization of the Psalms in Christian worship continued right up until the Wesleyan revival in the eighteenth century, when the new hymnody began to supplant the Psalter.[8]

---

7. See *De Musica* in *Augustine Through the Ages: An Encyclopedia*, ed. Allan D. Fitzgerald (Grand Rapids: Eerdmans, 1999), 572-76.

8. This should not be interpreted as a rejection of all modern hymns. George Matheson's "O Love, That Wilt Not Let Me Go" (Glasgow, 1842) is particularly close to my heart.

3

Ecclesial Betrayals of the Middle Ages

There is a correlation between obligatory celibacy and child abuse. The Orthodox Church allows its priests to marry although there remains a rumor of widespread child abuse. But it is a pandemic in the Roman Catholic Church, possibly from its origins. ("Celibacy" is traceable to Roman culture.) The word "celibacy" derives from the Latin *caelibatus*, which is used by Cicero, Seneca, Suetonius, and other Roman philosophers in referring to the unmarried state of men and women. But it was a voluntary choice when Jesus called his disciples (Matt. 19:12) and likewise in the early Church (1 Cor. 9:5; Titus 1:6; 1 Tim. 3:2-3). The first institutional steps were taken at the Council of Elvira (c. 306), which called upon bishops, priests, and deacons to refrain from having sexual relations with their wives and to have no children. But only following the Second Lateran Council in 1139 did the Latin Church fully adopt this rule. But in the centuries that followed, celibacy exerted heavy emotional stresses on the clergy in the form of loneliness, depression, and alcoholism—a secret world within the church community. Thus was the way opened to sexual abuse.[1]

Sexual Betrayal of Children

By the eleventh century we begin to hear voices recounting the sexual abuse of children. Two papal reformers, Peter Damien (c. 1007-1073) and Anselm of Bec (c. 1033-1109) hint at it as a personal experience, while Guibert of Nogent (c. 1055-1124) is fully explicit. In his Monodiae or "Solitary Songs" he tells of the constraining circumstances of his childhood.[2] Clearly, the reform of the Benedictine monastic order by Bernard of Clairvaux (1090-1153) that only accepted adult monks reflected this radical change in monastic recruitment. There is evidence that the growth of hermitages was a device to protect against sexual abuse. Julian of Norwich (1343-1416) is such an example. She had herself walled into a cloister whose window overlooked the church services to enable her to participate in the worship of the community, while a small hole opened to the street that enabled women to whisper to her their needs and receive her counsel. Such entomb-

---

1. *The Encyclopedia of Christianity*, vol. 1, ed. Erwin Fahlbusch et al. (Grand Rapids: Eerdmans, 1999), 38.

2. Quoted from J. M. Houston, "The Child in the Early Middle Ages," in James M. Houston, ed., *An Introduction to Child Theology* (Eugene, OR: Wipf & Stock, 2021).

ment also reflected the womb of Mary that gave birth to the Son of God.

Once, while teaching on the subject of child theology, a husband and wife told me they had a summer home in the mountains. Casually, I asked where. Almost hysterical, she told me she would not tell me or anyone else! Suddenly I realized she had suffered severe sexual child abuse, and this distant summer home was a safe place for her.

Alas, the celibacy of Roman Catholic priests has generated endemic child abuse for at least a millennium. It is a terrible betrayal![3]

The Betrayal of Communal Worship

Believers in Christ are called to be priests, kings, and the holy people of God (1 Pet. 2:9; Rev. 1:6; 5:10; 20:6). The early church held fast to the priesthood of all baptized believers, but in the early Middle Ages, there crept in the distinction between "the ordained" and "the laity." In turn this influenced changes in church architecture, beginning with the baroque in Notre Dame Cathedral in Paris, which was begun in 1163 and completed in 1345. Unity of space reflect-

---

3. Of course I am not implying that the majority of Catholic priests are guilty of the heinous crime of child sexual abuse. The frequency of this crime and its betrayal may also have increased with changing sexual mores since the 1960s. There is a voluntary, chaste, and even a joyous priestly celibacy.

ed the *corpus Christi* all being members of one body. But unlike the architectural simplicity of the Cistercian churches, the new cathedrals became far more ornate, and separation of priestly worship from the worship of the laity crept in with a curtain or paneled wall between them. Then there developed peripheral chapels for the prayers of mediation from Mary, the Mother of God, and from the mediation of favorite saints that over time were added.

Years ago, I was deeply challenged as I read the Nobel Prize winner William Golding's novel, *The Spire*. As a schoolmaster in Salisbury, Golding (1911-1993) could see in the distance the great spire of Salisbury Cathedral, the theme of his novel. The novel portrays the deep treachery of the Dean of the cathedral who desires to build a second and grander spire, not for the glory of God but for his own. It is an ironic story of how this medieval cleric insisted on building this second spire when the master of works protested it was a miracle that the first remained sustained on swampy land! But his technical expertise was overruled by the hubris of the Dean. In the tensions that follow, instead of being "a house of worship" it becomes one of intrigue and even of murder. The spire was built, but at the end of his life, Dean Jocelin confessed: "I thought I was chosen, a spiritual man, loving above all; and given specific work to do. And from this the rest followed, the debts, the deserted church, discord."[4] It has been a powerful warning to me ever since I read it. The grandiose edifices of the cathedrals often expressed the hubris of their founders.

It is a message that has sobered me ever since. Today we plan and then build new churches, only to see them disintegrate with clashing ideals, the different personalities of our church leaders, and bewildered, divided congregations. Like the story of *The Spire*, such schismatic divisions among Christians today are no different from those described by William Golding. Houses of prayer stop praying! "Worship" becomes an empty word!

But now we return to the history of building cathedrals. In the Renaissance, a Platonic idealism developed in the pontifical cathedral of Rome as the Church came to use the cathedral as an exhibition of the painting and sculpture of skilled artists such as G. Bernini (1598-1680), Michelangelo (1475-1564), and F. Borromini (1599-1667). They all were evoking a sense of Platonic infinity in the body of the edifice. Yes, these magnificent cathedrals evoked a sense of wonder and praise, as they still do. But they also distracted the simple worshipper, as now they appear simply as tourist attractions.

4. William Golding, *The Spire* (London: Faber & Faber, 1964), 194.

The Betrayal of Medieval Cathedral Worship

When Jerome translated the Bible into Latin in the fourth century there began "the tyranny of the Vulgate." The common people were excluded from personal access to the Bible, except for their daily singing of the Psalms. Later, when the cathedrals were built, a barrier was placed separating the area where the congregants worshipped from where the clergy worshipped. It was as if there was a reversal in the structure of the Jewish temple in Jerusalem. With chanting and singing in Latin, the worship of the people was largely excluded.

The role of the laity was confession to the priest, or offering simple prayers to the saints, usually by use of the rosary, not by articulated prayer. For many if not most female confessors, the priests were far too probing of their sexual lives; more details probably of which even their husbands knew. This became a long, ongoing abuse until women began to rebel, just in these last few decades. It has put off so many from church attendance.

Now, as was demonstrated recently with the fire of Notre Dame Cathedral in Paris, there was national consternation about the destruction of a cathedral. But as a national icon, much like the Eiffel Tower, the dismay was largely because it was a national monument for the tourists to visit. Indeed, all our medieval cathedrals in Western Europe are merely medieval marvels of architecture for tourists to visit, while their music also, as played by the ancient organs, is merely an aesthetic delight to those who love music. The pious generosity of its original worshippers, to put up such monuments of faith, helped by the widow's mite, has all but been forgotten. Our cathedrals are great monuments of the grand betrayal of Western Christianity.[5]

---

5. Even in these days God still speaks in these sacred spaces.

4

The Betrayals of the Reformation

In the fifteenth century the Iberian Peninsula remained on the fringe of Europe. It had been visited by the Phoenicians and Greeks, then overrun by the Romans and later by the Visigoths and the Arabs. In the south, al-Andalus developed as a society of half a million farmers and silk producers. With the Muslim invasion, it evolved into an Islamic culture. To the center and north, there developed a Christian culture of some six million souls, many migrants from Western Europe who had travelled to participate in the Crusades against the Muslims to the south. At an early stage it looked as if all of the Peninsula would be overrun by the burgeoning Muslim state. Christians lived under Muslim rule as "Mozarabes," and Muslims under Christian rule as "Mudejares." Living in Catalonia, Ramon Lull (d. c. 1315) composed a dialogue in which the three characters were a Christian, a Muslim, and a Jew. As Henry Kamen has documented in his book *The Spanish Inquisition*,[1] Muslims and Jews were far from being despised,

---

1. Henry Kamen, *The Spanish Inquisition* (New Haven: Yale University Press, 2014), 4.

enjoying a degree of social autonomy and coming together for community celebrations.

The Betrayal of Christian Unity in Spain

There were many Jewish Christians in Spain in the early Middle Ages. Probably the apostle Paul's desire to travel to "Tarsish," possibly Santander, would have followed an ancient copper and zinc trading route that is traceable to the Phoenician trade with the copper mines in Santander and tin from the peninsulas of Western Europe. This trade instituted the rise of the Bronze Age. Certainly, the diaspora of Jewish Christians in Spain continued to maintain the trade route until much later.

Beginning in 1232, and lasting until the nineteenth century, the Inquisition was a process developed by the Roman Church to detect baptized heretics and their supporters. Its activities were renewed in 1480 with the expulsion or forced conversion of Jews. It was a legal procedure of "inquiry" that began with civil crimes and then deepened into issues of religious faith, especially against the Jews.[2] Much later, in 1609, the expulsion of the Moriscos populated parts of the Balkans and generated later religious conflict after the world wars of the twentieth century. The Inquisition focused on torture to secure "voluntary confession," and on the death sentence by burning at the stake. It could be interpret-

2. Kamen, *The Spanish Inquisition*, 182.

ed as an ancient ecclesial organization having to adjust to changing culture and needing a uniformity that was increasingly seen as a legal necessity. It was based on the promotion of fear. Beginning in Spain in 1487, spreading into Portugal in 1536, and into Italy in 1542, its power was extended by the organization of spies to track down heretics. It was an *auto-da-fé*, that is, "a trial by faith." Individuals coming before the Inquisition included those accused of witchcraft or having relapsed into paganism, those being professedly Jewish Christians but practicing Judaism, and of course, those baptized Moors who had settled around irrigated gardens as migrants from North Africa but continued in Islam.[3]

Yet the Franciscan leaders were Jewish Christians, engaged in the reform of the Church, as was Queen Isabella's confessor, Cisneros, the Primate of Spain. Cardinal Garcia Cisneros composed a spiritual guide for Queen Isabella, *A Guide to the Spiritual Life*, in 1500. Deeply impressed, the pious Queen ordered Cisneros to build the city of Alcala de Henares in order to house a new university. It was there that scholars, including a young Dutch young scholar hired as a consultant, were assembled to produce the first translation of the Bible into the vernacular. Known as *El Libro del Oro*,

---

3. *The Eerdmans Encyclopedia of Christianity*, vol. 2, ed. Erwin Fahlbusch et al. (Grand Rapids: Eerdmans, 2001), 711-13.

"the Golden Book," it was published in 1511, a century before the King James Version.

Most of the Franciscan leaders that inspired the Spanish reformation begun by Cisneros in the early sixteenth century were Christian Jews, including Teresa of Avila, John of the Cross, and the Hebrew professor at the University of Salamanca, Luis de Leon. The latter spent a year in prison and was put on trial by the Dominican jurors of the Inquisition. During this time, John of the Cross was kidnapped and imprisoned in humiliating circumstances in the Dominican monastery in Toledo, until he escaped a year later.

Thus it is not popularly known that there was a Spanish Reformation before the German Reformation, which spread into Italy after 1531, led by Juan de Valdes, a refugee from the Spanish Inquisitors. Much later, Dostoyevsky echoes all this in his novel, *Brothers Karamazov*, where the Grand Inquisitor is himself being condemned for his worldly rule over Christendom.

The Betrayal of the Christian Identity

The political tensions between Spain, France, and England in the Tudor period challenged Queen Elizabeth (r. 1558-1603) to become a skilled diplomat. She developed the foreign policy of "the balance of power," both in relating to princely suitors desirous of a political liaison, as well as to creating three ecclesial parties within her domain as head of the church.

Ever since, the Church of England has been divided into three parties: the Anglo-Catholic, the Puritan-Presbyterian, and the Liberals, the most freethinking party that later promoted deism. The Anglo-Catholic party has always remained the most conservative. Following the era of great cathedral building was the Civil War in England under the Stuarts, which marks the deep division of identity between Puritan and Catholic. The Puritan movement was the vanguard of the Reformation, yet in mixed ways. A nickname of scorn, "the pure ones," the Puritans proudly preferred being called "Precisians," for "my God," they claimed, was "a precise God!" This was the birth of "systematic theology," which was the inheritance of Pierre Ramus, educational advisor to Louis XIV, and founder of the prestigious College de France. Truth, Ramus theorized, was discovered by the process of systemization, and like the tree of knowledge was divided into main and minor branches.

From this school of Ramus, some colleges in Oxford and Cambridge began to teach that even a sermon should be presented in such a dull fashion, and then when collated in commentaries, should still be so divided even more. Various colleges at Oxbridge followed this approach, creating lifeless expositions contained in biblical commentaries and sermons. This was a serious mockery of the Reformation cry, "By Scripture alone!"

Fortunately, some Puritans, trained at Emmanuel College, Cambridge, were secretly taught to express Scripture according to the Ignatian Exercises of the founder of the Jesuits, Ignatius of Loyola, and also the writing of Luis de Granada (1505-1568).[4] Their works remain lively expositions to this day. Thomas Watson (c. 1620-1686), in his writings on divinity, was familiar with the *Treatise on Prayer* of Luis de Granada, and this is reflected in his daily personal meditations on the Passion of our Lord, and in his promptitude for daily actions. Already Watson was putting his finger upon the betrayal that came through Christians in their failure to live devout lives. He asks: "Why are there so few Christians? Is it that people are so much in the shop that they are seldom on the mount with God?"[5] Even now, to read the writings of Watson, such as *The Art of Divine Contentment*, is to be personally refreshed and vitalized. For he was versed in the ancient practice of *lectio divina* (divine reading) but was also forward-looking in his understanding of the progress of science.

---

4. Emmanuel College had adopted, through trade links to the continent, this more liberal and dynamic approach.

5. Quoted by Norbert Haukenfrers, "Bellows of the Affections: The Meditative Spirituality of Thomas Watson," MCS thesis, Regent College, Vancouver.

Watson asks, "Why meditate?" For without it, religion becomes formality, tradition, and rules with no guiding relationship with which to see and understand the surrounding world. For "Godliness is the sacred impression of God in a man, whereby of carnal he is made spiritual. When godliness is wrought in a person . . . he hath another spirit." The Christian "becomes fixed to the immoveable God." And this fixing "is an intrinsical thing; it lies chiefly in the heart." Yet, godliness is also "an extensive thing: it is the sacred leaven that spreads itself into the whole soul."[6] He concludes: "Godliness is a permanent thing, supernatural and a glorious thing, as a precious jewel in a ring, so is piety to the soul, bespangling it in God's eyes. Reason makes us men, godliness makes us earthly angels."[7]

Watson's meditations on The Lord's Prayer, and his 176 sermons on the Westminster Shorter Catechism published in 1692, established him in the highest rank among the Puritans. The revival of his writings might much embarrass contemporary writing on systematic theology! Yet at the same time, it might wondrously renew our hearts in recovering a meditative way of life.

But alas. In the following Stuart period lesser minds quarreled with each other, as Richard Greaves has dark-

---

6. Haukenfrers, "Bellows of the Affections," 80.
7. Haukenfrers, "Bellows of the Affections," 80.

ly portrayed in his book, *Saints and Sinners*.[8] Then in the civil war that followed, there loomed the doctrine of the divine right of monarchs to be head of the state church. Then followed a whole sequence of identities related to the colonization of North America. Thomas Hobbes promoted "the monarchical self," the idea that we are all monarchs, analogous to the later "priesthood of all believers." Then at the end of the eighteenth century, John Locke promoted "the proprietorial self," the idea that the colonist who clears the forest and drains the swamps on the American coast has a right to its ownership. In turn, this sparked off the revolt of the English colonists against a haughty English Parliament.

Across the channel in France, Jean Jacques Rousseau wrote his novel *Emile*, reflecting the injustice given him by his stepmother as a child. Eventually such embers of discontent burst into revolutionary fire. The "self-conscious self" aroused the French Revolution. Led by urban "citizens," it was joined by peasants who were misjudged by their aristocratic landowners. That it did not spread into England is thanks to the revivalist campaigns of John Wesley, though he did rebel against the Anglican bishops.

Later in 1831, the French observer Alexis de Tocqueville, in his travels in the United States, observed

8. Richard Greaves, *Saints and Rebels* (Macon, GA: Mercer University Press, 1985).

there an interesting social experiment that he termed "the rise of the individual."

After World War II, the enormous potential of productivity, combined with the new, unprecedented challenge of "turning war machines into ploughshares" saw an expanded newspaper industry. With these newspaper and magazine empires came a voracious advertising industry that in turn spurred the illusion of "the empty self" that therapeutically now needed "self-fulfillment." Shopping malls, credit cards, and a multiplicity of professional identities with their new addictions have followed, to where we are now, far away from having a "Christian identity."

Even as Christians, we may not realize what a terrible betrayal our Christian identity now is, in contrast to the original teaching of the apostle Paul that our identity is "in Christ." Sadly, we have to confess we have betrayed our Christian identity.

5

Deism as the Betrayal of Christian Faith

Like all betrayals, deism began in small ways. It was first identified in 1564 by the Swiss reformer Pierre Viret, arising from the growth of astronomy. In some minds, God was now the eternal clockmaker who no more interfered in creation than does a clockmaker with his new instrument of time. In 1696 in England, John Toland published his controversial book, *Christianity Not Mysterious*, in which this mind-set is displayed.

Betrayal of the Creator

The concept of "nature" was an Aristotelian idea, and attached to it was the notion that nature was purposeful. This idea reemerged strongly in 1605 with Francis Bacon's book *The Advancement of Learning*. This occurred contemporaneously within a circle of Puritans that included Bishop Boyle, who came together to form the Royal Society of London for Improving Natural Science. Having contributed "Boyle's Law on Gas Propulsion," Boyle now reacted to the new deistic strain, as seen in Bacon, with a strong apologetic treatise entitled *Free Enquiry into the Vulgarily Receiv'd Notion of "Nature"* in 1686. Bacon was making a plea for the "separation of science and religion" precisely when Boyle and his friends were seeking to see science as being founded on biblical faith! Thomas Watson, like Boyle, saw creation as glorious to behold and profitable to study and meditate upon. Watson had a far grander realm of meditation than we Christians have today as exhibited in the following quotation: "[T]he Creation is but a theatre to act the great work of redemption upon. The world is a field, the Saints are the corn, the ordinances are the showers, the mercies of God are the showers that ripen the corn, death is the sickle that cuts it down, the Angels are the harvesters that carry it into the barn . . . God would never have made this field, were it not for the corn growing in it."[1] Thus Watson saw that "God has given us not only the book of the Scriptures . . . but the book of Creation . . . to show much of." In short, Boyle and Watson were singing with the Psalms while Bacon was Aristotelian and had betrayed biblical faith.

Voltaire's Deism

But it was Voltaire who pushed deism hardest after the Lisbon earthquake that struck on All Saints' Day,

---

1. Thomas Watson, *Gleanings from the Writings of Thomas Watson* (Soli Deo Gloria, 1997).

1755. On this annual celebration, the churches were packed with worshippers, especially within the central cathedral, when a disastrous earthquake struck. There followed a tsunami in the river Tagus nearby. One third of the city population perished, killed by falling heavy masonry or by drowning. "God has betrayed us" was the message of Voltaire in Paris, as it was precisely the devout who were the victims. The indifferent God of deism became an abstraction, just as today many have stumbled, having lost faith in a god who does not answer anguished prayers for a loved one dying of a deadly disease. The cry continues: "Why is God silent?"

As the "Age of Reason" unfolded with the growth of science in the seventeen and eighteenth centuries, so deism expanded. A "natural religion" developed corresponding with the "natural sciences." The aim was to be freed of all religious "superstition" and to be an outlook accessible to all people. With it grew an autonomous morality that was independent of revelation, as Immanuel Kant was to develop systematically.[2]

Kant's "Disappearance of Moral Knowledge"

Immanuel Kant (1724-1804) was the great architect of moralism, built on three elements: rationalism, empiricism, and moral activism. The *Critique of Pure*

2. H. Reventlow, *The Authority of the Bible and the Rise of the Modern World* (Minneapolis: Fortress, 1984), 289-410.

Reason, published in 1781, laid out his theoretical philosophy, popularized soon after by his *Prolegomena to Any Future Metaphysics*. Kant sought to counter the thought of David Hume (1711-1776), who had linked skepticism with empiricism. Kant's lasting importance was the building of the foundations of modern secular philosophy. Following René Descartes (1596-1650), Kant, especially in his second edition of *Critique of Pure Reason* (1787), attempted to embrace the totality of knowledge. Morals are based on reason, and reason is determined empirically in order to reinforce morals.

Soon after, Friedrich Hegel (1770-1831) twisted his rationalistic theory such that it became so complex as to make it impossible to define Hegelianism. Yet he was a Lutheran clergyman who preached his sermons to congregants who must have wondered what he was talking about. But the threefold composition of the school, the law, and the state were the main themes of his teaching.

From religion flowed politics, and from politics came the law of the state. All this was a substitution for the medieval theory of "the divine right of kings" as the religious premise of monarchical rule. But instead of "law" stemming from monarchical rule, it now came from "natural law" as the philosophy of the state. This in turn originated from "the philosophy of spirit," which was absolute since it was composed of both "the objective" and "the subjective." All this then flowed forward once more into "logic" or "law." No wonder it becomes almost incomprehensible and impossible for writers and readers alike to penetrate and understand the worldview of Hegelianism!

6

The Betrayal of Christion Emotions

After the incomprehensibleness of Hegelianism, things got even worse with the thinking of Friedrich Schleiermacher. Boldly, he sought to reconstitute Christianity on purely rationalistic terms. Schleiermacher (1768-1834) was another son of a Lutheran pastor—a Prussian military chaplain to be precise. At Berlin, Schleiermacher acquired "free thinking" ideas, influenced by the Jewish Dutch philosopher Spinoza and by his study of Plato. Involved with Alexander Humboldt in the refounding of the University of Berlin after Napoleon's closing of it, he mixed the Lutheran pietism he had learned in the University of Halle with the skepticism of Spinoza. His published sermons fill seven volumes.

Schleiermacher possessed a great breadth of knowledge in philosophy and theology, combined with the new disciplines of psychology, linguistics, and anthropology. Through this polyglot lens, he taught that religion was not primarily a matter of holding concepts, ideas, and doctrines; these were secondary. What was constitutive was experience. Schleiermacher proclaimed: "Christian doctrines are accounts of the Christian religious affections set forth in speech."[1] Thus his early Pietism now concealed half-truths and half-lies. Now he too, like Hegel, wanted to reconstitute Christianity on purely rationalistic categories.

Schleiermacher's lens is a betrayal of the dimension of the personal. It has become as antiquarian as a pair of old shoes, unfit to walk in. Yet it added further dynamism to the rise of secularism. The Enlightenment had shifted from Western to Northern Europe and was now all "Lutheran." Why?

To seek the answer we need to go back to Martin Luther's own teaching. Martin Luther (1483-1546) would not have survived without the protection of German princes, while John Calvin (1509-1564) was protected by the city council of the free city of Geneva. From the beginning of his reform movement Luther made compromises: first in his adverse prejudice toward the Jews, which Hitler immediately added to his political agenda after coming to power in 1933, and then in "the doctrine of the two kingdoms." Such antinomies marked his whole career. Luther was a Catholic monk who married, already a youthful reformer before the Reformation, in constant conflict with other reformers, and the leader of a popular mass movement.

---

1. Friedrich Schleiermacher, *The Christian Faith*, trans. H. R. Mackintosh and J. S. Stewart (London: T&T Clark, 1999), §15.

In contrast, Calvin possessed a more personal stance. But most critical of all, Luther "rendered to Caesar the things that are Caesar's, and to God the things that are God's." Lutheran movements became state movements across all of northern Europe. Always there was compromise between the role of religion and the governance of the state.

In the twentieth century this ambiguity developed fully into the university teaching of theology to the point that to be academically "objective" about the study of theology, tenured professors really had to be non-believers of their discipline. This outlook has now spilled over into Oxford University where the former Vicar (for thirty years) of University Church exhibits nonbelief in his book *Christian Atheist: Belonging Without Believing*.[2] It boggles the mind what would happen to all our other professional disciplines if they followed this premise. This is, of course, the discourse of "comparative religion" such that the chairs of theology at Oxford, endowed by royal assent at the Reformation, are gradually all disappearing into the amalgam of comparative religion. If this happened to a private estate today, the lawyers of the estate would be charged with criminal offence.

2. Brian Mountford, *Christian Atheist: Belonging Without Believing* (Alresford: John Hunt, 2011).

But we have to retrace our steps to the Lutheran response of the young genius Søren Kierkegaard (1813-1855) in light of the tragedy of deism. In place of abstraction, he sought to recover "the person," which is why he later became known as "the father of existentialism." This is a misnomer, for he was against all "-isms," seeing them as forms of reductionism.

Growing up in what today we would call a dysfunctional family, Kierkegaard was the seventh child of a well-to-do wool merchant in Copenhagen. At the age of seventeen, while studying philosophy and theology in the university, his mother died. A young Søren was never able to escape his father's overwhelming guilt and depression, for his father had had an affair with a maidservant. Søren so concealed his father's betrayal of his mother that he broke off his own engagement to his fiancé Regine because he could not share with her "this dark secret." He was left all alone, as the first five of his siblings had died, and then his father in 1838. These circumstances caused him to fiercely react to his Danish culture whose "law of Jante" was "thou shalt not be different from anybody else!" Like a lonely fir tree standing in the flat Jutland landscape, Kierkegaard fiercely defied his culture and the conventional Christendom around him with brilliant treatises. These were of two types: some identified him as the author, and others were anonymous. Following Socratic dialogue he saw human progress as unfinished business. Through his writing, Kierkegaard succeeded in escaping from the crowd to become a defiant person.

"Truth" he defines as dialogical, and by doing so vehemently denies the abstractions of his Lutheran predecessors. Rather, "truth" concerns human life and all its emotions. Likewise faith is "lived" personally, both emotionally and rationally. Like no other prophet of the emotions before or since, Kierkegaard passionately proclaimed that to be "a Christian person," one must be healed and substantiated. Then Christian growth, that is personal growth, destroys the abstraction of "Christendom." At the end of his life, his final outburst against the state church, *Against Christendom*, outraged his fellow citizens, as it was a demolition of their whole society and culture—all they stood for.

The Betrayal of Contemporary Stoicism

In periods of pandemic fear, Stoicism has always appeared as a substitute emotion. It occurred after the pandemic of the "Black Death" or typhus, peaking in 1348, and in the next generation of Montaigne. It recurred after the plague and fire of London with Shakespeare as the dramatic Stoic. Cycles of fear and Stoicism have recurred several times since. Writ into the conduct of the military forces today is the ethics of Stoicism.

"Pyschologism," which lists all the emotions descriptively, has no reference to the healing of the emotions. We have to go back to the early fathers to read about such healing of the emotions.[3] But we do have illustrious Christians like Juan de Valdes in the sixteenth century, and then in the seventeenth century, Blaise Pascal and Cardinal Fenelon. But above all, in the nineteenth century lived the prophet of the Christian emotions, Søren Kierkegaard, who profoundly penetrated into the basic negative emotions of fear and depression.

Today, living in a global pandemic of fear like no other, Søren Kierkegaard has become the prophetic healer of our wounded emotions.[4]

Friedrich Nietzsche (1844–1900)

But in the flow of history no one has "the last word." If anyone could express most violently "the last betrayal," it was Friedrich Nietzsche. In the generation following Schleiermacher and Kierkegaard, Nietzsche is the modern prototype of Judas Iscariot. In his father we see, once again, a Lutheran pastor. He was a weak, sickly man who died when Nietzsche was not yet five. Nietzsche illustrates the betrayal of inverted morality, just

---

3. See Pia Sophia Chaudhari, *Dynamis of Healing: Patristic Theology and the Psyche* (New York: Fordham University Press, 2019).

4. James M. Houston, *Thesaurus of Christian Emotions*, forthcoming.

as Judas Iscariot interpreted Jesus as a weak messiah who was betraying Israel by his submissive acceptance of death on a Roman cross. So too Nietzsche saw Jesus not acting as a superman but as a weakling. Actually, Nietzsche was acting out compensatory behavior against his own deceased father and against his mother and younger sister, both of whom were strong women. But Nietzsche was highly dangerous, as he diabolically inspired Adolf Hitler to become the Superman of the German race. Like Goebbels after him, Nietzsche had the skills of a brilliant stylist, a subtle psychologist, a biting critic of "the status quo," and a pamphleteer. Like Schleiermacher, in putting himself on the side of "feeling, instinct, will, and hate," he exerted profound influence on our past generation.

7

The Modern Betrayal of Capitalism

Capitalism has had many betrayals. The first was by a universal slavery that the ancient world assumed to be a natural institution. It reached its apogee within Roman civilization, which could not have been sustained without it. Atlantic slavery came in the wake of the European voyages of discovery in the sixteenth century, and especially with the investment of capital in Brazil and in the Caribbean islands. Its links with sugar production were intrinsic, for sugar cane loses half of its sucrose content within twenty-four hours of cutting. Being labor intensive, the plantation estate required many slaves living close by for harvesting and processing. The dark stain of slavery lingered on in the history of its nations. It explains many revolts, beginning with the Haitian Revolution of 1791, carrying through to Fidel Castro and the Cuban Revolution, and elsewhere in Latin America.[1]

---

1. However, it should not be forgotten that slavery was present within aboriginal cultures, in varying degrees, prior to contact

A second betrayal of capitalism was in the making of the Industrial Revolution, when child labor was exploited in the coalmines and in the factories manufacturing cotton cloth. But it took a long time for these betrayals to be recognized, for even Martin Luther accepted the traditional evaluation of slavery. Only some Quakers, Mennonites, and eventually Methodists preached against it.

It was the Clapham Sect led by William Wilberforce (1759-1833) that achieved the momentum needed to start a revolt against the slave trade, beginning with a campaign "to reform the manners of the aristocracy." Parliament followed with reform in the acts of 1807 and 1834. It was a huge political task. But in the United States slavery splintered churches in 1845, 1857, and in 1863, eventually leading to the Civil War (1861-1865). While slavery has largely been abolished in the Western world today, workers too often remain exploited.

A third betrayal of capitalism was Marxism. Karl Marx (1818-1883) held that morality is not deduced from Christian principles but purely from the ideological reflections of the current culture. This is class determined as a form of historicism, and thus materialistic. Marx wrote voluminously on his theory of money as

---

with Europeans, even if it was Europeans who routinized the institution making it more "efficient".

value in motion rather like the hydrological cycle, defining new terms as he unfolded his theory. First, the social labor we do for others is organized through commodity exchanges as competitive, price-fixing markets. Second, Marx defines value as socially necessary time. It acts like gravity does in the hydrological cycle. We use "value" all the time as we relate it to political power, historical materialism, national identity, and the like. Money is the material representation of this power. The capitalist goes into the marketplace and buys two kinds of commodity: labor power and the means of production. No longer does the owner buy the laborer, as he once bought his slaves, but rather the owner buys daily fixed hours of work. The means of production are commodities much like automotive parts, silicon chips, and factory machines as well as the surrounding transport infrastructures, such as roads, railways, sewage, and water and electric power.

The integration of the means of production entails the use of technologies, an issue that looms large in Marx's definition, and it is constantly changing. Marx here identifies a paradox that the more sophisticated is the technology, the less is the labor congealed in the individual commodity produced. But the value of labor power varies from place to place and over time, so how does one create a certain standard of living? Reflecting on the hidden abode of production, Marx discovered that there is in capitalist production both the production in use and the production in surplus, all benefiting the capitalist. This tension has become exacerbated with time, and this is the dynamic that Marx sought to reform. Surplus should not go on relentlessly, going more and more into the pockets of the capitalist. Wage labor, redistribution of money, social goods, and taxes and tithes all demanded reform.[2]

Marx accepted the theory of Adam Smith's "hidden hand," but he did not see this building utopia in the market but dystopia. For Adam Smith, as a Christian, the "hidden hand" was the act of divine providence. For Marx there was no divine providence, indeed no God. Sadly, Marx was right about the persistence of much human greed that did, and still does, create dystopia. But we will not explore the intricacies of Marx's theory, which would distort the purpose of this book. We simply conclude that Marxist theory demands that the national state should control the unrestricted flow of supply and demand—not the church, monarchy, or aristocracy.

The fuse for the Russian Revolution was now in place. Within Marxism and then in later versions of it—revised by such leaders as Engels, Trotsky, and above all Lenin (1870-1924)—religion came to be

2. See David Harvey, *Marx, Capital, and the Madness of Economic Reason* (Oxford: Oxford University Press, 2018).

viewed as "spiritual alcohol." Marxism now demanded atheism as the sine qua non of being a Marxist.

Today, capitalism seems a very mild affair. But as it has been critiqued by Georg Simmel (1858-1918) in *The Philosophy of Money* (1900), it too reveals its treachery. For money is amoral in itself, but as it is used it becomes highly moral. But for Simmel, as a youth, it became a matter of life or death as he was wounded by a gunshot triggered by a desperate debtor who tried to kill him. So the study of money became a life-long one for this lecturer in sociology at the University of Berlin. Yet he was a stranger in the academy, snubbed by his colleagues, and his writings on the psychology of money were ignored. That is why he was truly a biblical prophet in the new realm of the expanding professions in the nineteenth century.

Simmel was continuously engaged in coming to terms with the three disciplines of philosophy, history, and sociology. He saw philosophy as having two tasks: first to deal with the basic concepts and presuppositions that underlie concrete research, and second, the speculative rounding out of the results of research and the efforts to integrate them into a total picture.[3]

According to Simmel, the discipline of history is that way of ordering the world which selects certain

---

3. Georg Simmel, *The Philosophy of Money*, trans. Tim Bottomore and David Frisby (New York: Routledge, 2011).

contents that have already been shaped in human experience. Selection is crucial, for history then creates a world of its own, self-contained and commensurable.

The newer discipline of sociology has its roots elsewhere. It derives from the ascendancy of the masses over the interests of individuals, seeks to discern the varying social classes of humanity, and then study all that is going on within these classes: the rich and the poor, the spendthrift and the greedy, the aristocrat and the peasant, the public and the hidden—like the Jew in a culture of anti-Semitism. Yet Simmel also sees the need to particularize individuals within society, such that sociology does not become a social abstraction.[4] Instead, it examines "money," as Simmel interprets it, as an agent of exchange. In place of a hoarding and robbing economy, as it was with the Vikings and the Normans in the tenth and eleventh centuries, it is now an amicable exchange of goods.

With this exhaustive intellectual background, Simmel then outlined his philosophy of money. But the emphasis on money also comes with a loss of transcendent values, although ironically, our secular society now worships money as if it were a god. For it replaces transcendence with imminent values such as greed, envy, and other negative emotions. As such it becomes

---

4. Levine, ed., *Georg Simmel*, xxiv-xxv.

a competitive value. Indeed, it becomes amoral, with a low sense of the needs of others. This lack of a dialectic of inwardness between a concern for one's self and an outward concern for others generates the inwardness of mimesis or imitation of others.

This lack of concern for the "other" then generates "fashion," which is derived from the bent desire for novelties. Its attraction is empowered by money in order to create power over others. The inflation of money then follows, along with the piling up of national debt and other negative consequences of social alienation. It presents a bleak picture for the world's democracies at two levels: first are the destructive consequences of social alienation as seen in the presence of beggars and homeless in our streets. But second, and more chilling, is the threat of the huge economy of China buying up American debt and becoming the most powerful economy in the world. This Simmel did not live to see, but he knew all the consequences of human greed.

Fortunately, the rise of major charitable organizations to assist the world's poorest nations are beacons of the light of being "human." Enlightened taxation of Western wealth provides tax credit for donations to such charities. Simmel was the nineteenth-century prophet against abstraction, alienation, and abstract aesthetics. Yet who knows Simmel today! Even the highly esteemed *Encyclopedia of Christianity* has an article on "money" but no reference to Georg Simmel. It is as if he has disappeared from the historical record, and his absence is a great loss . . . and a great critique of history.

8

The Betrayal of Christian Aesthetics

What does the word aesthetic mean? The question is not one of definition but of discovery and identification. The Greek word *aesthesis* denotes sensation or perception. It is the antithesis of seeking for ends, as capitalism has sought, for it is about ways of perception. It seeks clarity, even in the mystery of ends. It is about the realm of value that is incarnated, inviting us in to appreciate and enjoy like a festival, yet to enjoy it critically as we may enjoy a poem. It is like having good manners.

What then is "art"? The German philosopher Eugen Rosenstock-Huessy (1888-1973) defines it as "an imitation of the lovable—it plays with the lovable. The strong is not lovable and the frail is. Art is love at play." Again he observes: "To be artistic means to be able to see the world today as though it never had existed before. The artist is that eye and ear and taste of the first wonder at the dawn of creation. Art is the dream of humanity's spring, eternally young, eternally surprising."[1]

This lyricism about good art is so contrastive to modern art. As we shall see the betrayal of the aesthetic has come on a long regress since the Renaissance artists.

What Is the Purpose of "Good Art"?

From this understanding of the aesthetic it follows that "good art disturbs the comfortable, and comforts the disturbed." It has a prophetic role to play in society, as "a speech in painting." One thinks of the famous painting "Guernica" by Picasso, in the Prado art gallery of Madrid, that depicts all the horrors of the Civil War, or contrastively, the still art of Rembrandt that depicts all the good things of creation.

Georg Simmel's *Rembrandt* (1916) explores the inner life of humanity within the single biography of an artistic genius. Indeed, Rembrandt (1606-1669) teaches the Christian Gospel in art, as his portraits depict: "The Holy Family" (1634); "Christ Healing the Sick" (1649); "Christ and the Samaritan Woman" (1659); "The Return of the Prodigal Son" (c.1668); St. John the Baptist Teaching" (c.1668); "The Preaching of Jesus" (c.1652); "The Entombment of Jesus" (an etching, c. 1654); "Christ at Emmaus" (1648).

---

1. Eugen Rosenstock-Huessy, *Lifelines: Quotations from His Works*, ed. Clinton C. Carver (Norwich, VT: Argo, 1988), 1.

As Simmel interprets Christian aesthetics, the facts of history are interwoven with the inner life of the Christian. The outer life of the Christian, made in the image and likeness of God, is a witness to creation. This transcendent reality is reflected by the immanent presence of God in becoming Christlike. Hence the whole purpose of Rembrandt's art is to inspire us to become and grow as a "Christian person." It is to concretize in daily life, "becoming more and more a Christian." Likewise, in Leonardo da Vinci's painting "The Last Supper," there is depicted the consternation of the religiosity of the banquet party in hearing the words of Jesus: "One of you will betray me." As I said at the beginning of this book, this is the question that I hear at every sacramental meal.

Christian art is therefore the unity of the soul of man with the heart of God. Betrayal of Christian aesthetics begins, then, with leaving out Christ from human art. There then follows the loss of hope, and the end result becomes the disintegration of the future in a secularized humanity.

The Eclipse of Christian Aesthetics in Art

As it is with money, aesthetics too has many facets. It reflects the primordial betrayal of Adam and Eve in their rebellion against their creator, for they used their eyes to see the forbidden fruit and were seduced by the serpent. Since then, for countless millennia, we have seen, in Paul's words, "through a glass darkly" (1 Cor. 13:12).[2]

Only when the Venetian traders began to import glass to Venice did they find a better refractory glass in the Po delta at Murano. Now they could see themselves "face to face." The French aristocracy in the seventeenth century then went crazy over the new glass, spending fortunes to have their chateaux and palaces outfitted with floor-to-ceiling mirrors. The self-conscious philosophy of J. J. Rousseau added intensity to what became so central to French philosophy in the nineteenth to twentieth centuries: existentialism. It has become a great betrayal of aesthetics!

In sharp contrast, as we have seen with Rembrandt, the Dutch Reformation produced great artists who celebrated creation in "still art," with a bowl of cherries or other fruit so vividly depicted. Better still, the human portraits are focused upon the human eye, as if the apostle's prediction was being partially fulfilled: seeing ourselves face to face, as one day we shall see the glory of the Lord.

But gradually the betrayal of aesthetics began with the influence of deism. In the twentieth century, much modern art has lost the realism of landscapes and hu-

---

2. Paul is referring to the primitive glass mirrors invented by the Phoenicians, not far from Paul's hometown of Tarsus.

man portraiture, devolving into a morass of abstractions that more reflect the artist's mind than the real world around us. Now there is no hint of the religious past, no awareness of worshipping "in the beauty of holiness." Rather art has become "art for art's sake," for the worship of money and egotism. It no longer sees "with the eye" but "through the eye," as the engraver Hogarth had distinguished in the eighteenth century.

As Simmel links the analogies of money and aesthetics in his other book, *The Philosophy of Aesthetics*, we are reminded of the claims of Jesus: "I am the Way [of seeing reality], the Truth [of divine revelation], and the Life [everlasting]" (John 14:6). As he concludes, "The achievements of human history are shot through with a contrast that can be characterized as that between the capacity to create and the capacity to fashion . . . there is no human work, beyond pure imitation, that is not simultaneously fashioning and creating."[3]

It is as historic beings that we "create". Yet as spiritual beings, we become "trans-historical" beings. We are re-forming all the time. We need to do so with art, with thought, with spirit, with emotions, and with human institutions.

---

3. See Georg Simmel, *Rembrandt: An Essay in the Philosophy of Art*, ed. Alan Scott and Helmut Stubmann (Oxford: Routledge, 2005), 155.

The Betrayal of the Human Heart

But basic to all is the guarding of the human heart. We read the injunction in the book of Proverbs, "Above all else, guard your heart, for it is the fountain of life" (Prov. 4:23). An ancient meditation on the sacraments by Jacques de Vitry (*De Sacramentis*) states: "Just as we have died through the appetite in Adam, so shall we recover life through the taste of Christ, as whence arose death, thence shall life re-arise."

Man's expulsion from paradise is the discovery of his limitations, his loss of community, and of being bonded relationally. "Eating the apple" functions as an eye-opener of a heart betrayed by the serpent in the garden. The prophet Jeremiah is the Old Testament custodian of the heart of Israel. He observed: "The heart is perverse above all things and desperately wicked" (Jer. 17:9). Frequently he chides the Israelites as being betrayers of God's covenant "by the imagination of their hearts."

In his *Manual for Interior Souls*, the Jesuit J. N. Grou states our fallen condition very clearly:

> This perverse and corrupt element in our nature is a consequence of original sin, which has led astray the primitive uprightness of our hearts, and has concentrated upon our own selves that affection which is to be given to God alone. If we observe ourselves carefully, we shall find we

love everything in proportion as it affects ourselves, that we judge of everything according to our own view of it, and solely with regard to our own interests: instead of which, we ought to love everything, and even ourselves, only in God and for God's sake. And the source of all our vices—those of the mind and of the heart, is that we will reverse this right order of things: this is the root of all our sins, and the sole cause of our eternal ruin.[4]

In a series of essays, Grou traces how the perversity of heart that the prophet Jeremiah describes, begins in one's childhood, and the Augustinian theme of "let me know Thee O God, let me know myself" is also Grou's pulse-beat. Likewise, Grou's focus is upon our living in "spiritual childhood," as Jesus calls us to be "as little children." Quoting Bossuet, a seventeenth century French bishop, he concludes with the latter's prayer: "Grant us all, as in becoming all as like little children, as Jesus Christ commanded us, we may enter ourselves once for all by this little door, and then may we be able to show others the way more surely and more efficaciously. Amen."[5]

---

4. J. N. Grou, *Manual for Interior Souls* (London: Burns Oates & Washbourne, 1892), 161.
5. Grou, *Manual*, 415.

9

The Moral Betrayal of Our Major Institutions

"Teach us to number our days, that we may apply our hearts unto wisdom" (Ps. 90:12). There is a fear today that the modern research university has been disintegrating since the early 1930s. The rapidity with which new universities and new professions were added after World War II has hastened the speed of their becoming demoralizing institutions. Max Weber predicted they would become "specialists without spirit." Then in 1987, Allan Bloom landed a bombshell titled *The Closing of the American Mind* on how higher education had failed democracy and impoverished the souls of its students. Universities had become educational factories.

Universities have now long lost the once sacred relationship between mentor and student that developed in the late medieval universities, such as Paris, Freiburg, Oxford, and Cambridge. Their colleges had been given names such as Jesus College, Corpus Christi, Trinity College, and All Soul's, for they were for the nurture of students' souls as well as the education of the mind.

When I was teaching at Oxford, our teachers of philosophy were mesmerized by the new fad of logical positivism that treated philosophy as a mere logical puzzle. Fortunately, there were such defenders of Christian education as C. S. Lewis (1898-1963). When I asked Lewis, at the end of his life, what was the summary of his writings, his response was "against reductionism." One of his last books, *Until We Have Faces*, was never popular, and Lewis scarcely persuaded his publisher to issue it. Another of his later writings was *The Abolition of Man*, and it also was published to little notice. But Lewis was arguing that there was no longer a robustness of morals in modern education, leaving its adherents "without chests."

Let me regress. Losing his mother when he was nine years old, then almost immediately sent by his father a "thousand miles away" from Belfast to a private school near London, Lewis later described the experience "as if Plato's continent of Atlantis, had slipped under the waves, leaving him swimming upon a dark ocean."

When struggling from atheism to deism in his early professional life, he writes to his friend Greeves: "[O]ne of the first results of my Theistic conversion, was a marked decrease of the fussy attentiveness which I had so long paid to the progress of my own opinions and the states of my mind . . . to believe and pray were the beginning of extroversion."

Later in his life, he had become a determined apologist for objectivism rather than subjectivism. This he summarized in *Till We Have Faces*, a rewriting of Ovid's myth.[1] It is a re-visioning of self, just as in the novel the sister, Psyche, has to die, her sister Orual, now the queen of the land, wears only a mask until she too follows Psyche to learn that it is only through death to the self that she too can have a "face." By the end of the book, Orual has no will, no pride, and no jealousy left in her; she is "unmade" in order to experience metanoia, a radical change of identity and being, in order to become "a person-in-Christ."[2] At the ending Oruel concludes: "I ended my first book with the words 'no answer.' I know now Lord, why you utter no answer. You are yourself the answer. Before your face questions die away. What other answer would suffice? Only words, words; to be led out to battle against other words. Long did I hate you, long did I fear you."[3] God's gift of human identity is contrastive with the secular educational process that Lewis called *The Abolition of Man*. This small book, Lewis told me, was the most im-

---

1. C. S. Lewis, *Till We Have Faces: A Myth Re-Told* (New York: Harper Collins, 2012).

2. See Sharon Jebb Smith, "C. S. Lewis: From Self-Obsession to Plerosis," in *Sources of the Christian Self*, ed. James M. Houston and Jens Zimmermann (Grand Rapids: Eerdmans, 2014), 603-17.

3. Lewis, *Till We Have Faces*, 351.

portant work he had written. Little did he know he was becoming a prophet against our robotic age of artificial intelligence. For in his age, he was focused upon the current philosophical fad of logical positivism.

Now our students come with intellectual curiosity, puzzled by the foundations of science, disturbed by religious questions, agonized over politics, captivated by literature and art. But they cannot hammer at the doors of their professors because they are closed, except for a brief timetable of "contact hours." The scandal is that this is not just happening in our secular universities but in our Christian universities and colleges. Bruce Wilshire, in his book *The Moral Collapse of the University: Professionalism, Purity and Alienation*, sees this professionalization and careerism as devastating.

Fortunately, we have our prophets from the past who denounced this educational betrayal. Notable was Charles Malik (1906-1975), the Lebanese philosopher who became first Minister of State, then Ambassador to the United States, followed by his election as the first President of the General Assembly of the United Nations. There, he served on the committee for the elaboration of the Universal Declaration of Human Rights. No one has had more honorary doctorates—some fifty—from distinguished universities. His book then, *A Christian Critique of the University*, is authoritative like no other. He begins this small book with the question:

"What does Jesus Christ think of the university?"[4] Passionately, Malik lays seven charges against this betrayal;

> The relentless expansion of knowledge as power: in molecular biology, nuclear physics, and other sciences, with scientists hostile to, or indifferent to, moral/spiritual values. The problem of wholeness, of order, not only in the sciences, but principally in concrete, existential, individual living. The marvels of modern transportation and communication. [And now we can add the "tech revolution" that has brought more diverse people together than ever before. But the gap between data processing and the communication of moral values grows ever wider. Conversation is about the weather, or, in the senior's home where I am now lodged, the menu for the next meal. —JMH]

The tremendous problem, states Malik, is "of whether there is essential incompatibility between reason and faith, between knowledge and virtue, between scholarship and the sense of mystery.... Can we give ourselves totally to Jesus Christ and the life of contemplation and create intellectually? ... It appears something must be sacrificed. We admire the accomplishments of the great scholars and philosophers, but we

---

4. Paraphrase of Charles Habib Malik, *A Christian Critique of the University* (Downers Grove, IL: InterVarsity Press, 1982), 95-97.

are not impressed by their spiritual state. They appear to lack grace, humility, contrition, love, joy, perhaps even feeling."[5]

Yet the university is the microcosm of the world. To reform it is much more than a new curriculum, or evangelizing efforts among students on the campus, or encouraging professors in their churches. It demands asking, Is the intellect to be totally dependent on or independent of Jesus Christ, to remain sound and sane and true?

Jesus Christ is the ultimate judge of all the earth. Are we therefore seeking his judgment of our human institutions by being unafraid to speak out boldly as his disciples?

We face a dilemma then: do we remain brave and stay within secular universities, or do we create new Christian universities, only to find that they too have become "double-agents," in the language of espionage? The only response Christians can make is to obey the apostolic commission: "to earnestly contend for the faith" (Jude 3).

An International Institute of Christian Scholarship

On a practical level, Malik was urging some of us, as his friends in Washington, DC, to create an Institute

5. Malik, *Christian Critique*, 99.

of Christian Studies that might act as an international world headquarters in order to promote the growth of Christian scholarship. He envisaged it to be rather like the World Council of Churches in Geneva, or even like the United Nations Commission in New York, which Malik himself had helped to found for the preservation of democracy. Was this thinking too big?

Dietrich Bonhoeffer (1906-1945) did not think so when he urged fellow believers to become "worldly Christians."[6] Malik appeals to the great philosophers, Socrates and Plato, groping as the apostle Paul sees them, "for the unknown God." (Acts 17:31). Malik quotes the Greek philosophers:

> *Stranger, appeals Plato.* But tell me, in heaven's name: are we really to be so easily convinced that change, life, soul, understanding have no place in that which is perfectly real [the Idea, the Form], that it has neither life, nor thought, but stands immutable in solemn aloofness, devoid of intelligence?
>
> *Theaetetus.* That sir, would be a strange doctrine to accept.
>
> *Stranger.* But can we say it has intelligence without having life?

---

6. See Jens Zimmermann, *Dietrich Bonhoeffer's Christian Humanism* (Oxford: Oxford University Press, 2019).

Theaetatus. Surely not.

Stranger. But if we say it contains both, can we deny that it has soul in which they reside?

Theaetatus. How else could it possess them?

It is life, life, real life, authentic life, eternal life, that all philosophers ultimately seek.

As Malik concludes, "How much Socrates, Plato and Aristotle would have rejoiced to hear Jesus say, "I am the Way, the Truth and the Life.""[7]

But today, scientists for the most part are naturalists; they worship nature. What about those personal problems with their families, their colleagues, or within themselves? What about their inner loneliness, depression, and alcoholism? If the university becomes "their home," and if the institution betrays their personal needs, how can they help their students facing worse problems that lie ahead of the next generation?

And what about the humanities that are engaged directly in studying the human condition? As Malik argues, "the fundamental spirit of the whole university is determined by the humanities." And the life of its teachers is even more decisive. In an academic crisis of my own life, when I once offered to resign, it was because my colleagues were making the distinction be-

---

7. Malik, *Christian Critique*, 63-64.

tween public morals and private lives; the Principal of our college in Oxford was highly acclaimed in the British government, but his private morals were in shambles. But for college expediency, they did not want to let him resign.

Eugen Rosenstock-Huessy, who taught at Harvard and then resigned to create his own intellectual community on his estate in Maine, stated: "If the university does not reform, it cannot perform. The university is the future of the country dealt with beforehand."[8]

Of course, he is so right, for if the university is an agent of reform of the mind, how will it ever do its task without constantly reforming itself? As he also stated, "A new form of thought must be lived first before it may be externalized into endowed institutions."[9]

The Betrayal of the National Press

The national press has never had an ethical code, as have other institutions, such as the judiciary, business corporations, and legal and accountant services. So the press has never had checks and balances, other than cases of defamation that might be brought to the courts. I have found no book prescribing ethics for

---

8. Eugen Rosenstock-Huessy, *Lifelines: Quotations from the Work of Eugen Rosenstock-Huessy*, ed. Clinton C. Gardner (Norwich, VT: Argo, 1988), 20.

9. Rosenstock-Huessy, *Lifelines*, 64.

journalists, although there are codes of conduct for its employees by their employers. Our press purports to be a "free press" as the voice of democracy. During the Second World War, Henry Luce, the publisher of *Time* and *Life* magazines, organized The Commission on Freedom of the Press to explore whether freedom of the press was in danger, and what was the proper function of the press in a free Democracy. The Commission warned:

> The modern press was a new phenomenon. Its typical unit is the great agency of mass communication. These can facilitate thought and discussion. They can stifle it. They can advance the progress of civilization or they can thwart it. They can debase and vulgarize mankind. They can endanger the peace of the world; they can do so accidentally in a fit of absence of mind. They can play up or down the news and its significance, foster and feed emotions, create complacent fictions and blind spots, misuse the great words, and uphold empty slogans. Their scope and power are increasing every day as new instruments become available to them. These instruments can spread lies faster and farther than our forebears dreamed when they enshrined the freedom of the press in the First Amendment to our Constitution.[10]

---

10. Commission on Freedom of the Press, *A Free and Responsible Press* (Chicago: University of Chicago Press, 1947).

Kovach and Rosentiel list the elements of journalism as follows:

- Journalism's first obligation is the truth.
- Its first loyalty is to citizens.
- Its essence is a discipline of verification.
- Its practitioners must maintain an independence from those they cover.
- It must serve as an independent monitor of power.
- It must provide a forum for public criticism and compromise.
- It must strive to make the news significant and interesting.
- It must keep the news comprehensive and in proportion.
- Its practitioners have an obligation to exercise their personal consciences.
- Citizens too have rights and responsibilities when it comes to news.[11]

What we are now seeing are the consequences of moral abstraction. Already pressing in upon us is an independent press "ideology" in the newsroom. Numerous journalists move from the newsroom to the agencies of national governance, such as the State Department, National Security, Congress, and the Sen-

---

11. Bill Kovach and Tom Rosenstiel, *The Elements of Journalism: What Newspeople Should Know and the Public Should Expect* (New York: Crown, 2014).

ate. In the contemporary revolt of the Youth in Hong Kong, why are there so many "journalists" mingled with the crowd?

How Did This All Come About?

The "press" was initiated in providing weekly articles on topics of current development in Edinburgh as a penny paper during the Age of Enlightenment, such as new ploughs, new forms of husbandry, sanitation, and so on. These articles were then collated into the first edition of the Encyclopedia Britannica in 1769.

Soon after, Fleet Street in London began to produce daily papers that advertised new shopping goods. Much later, with the invention of radio at the end of the nineteenth century, Lord Reid, the son of a Scottish Presbyterian minister, launched the B.B.C. radio, with the intent of improving the morals of the British public, as William Wilberforce had made his drive "to improve the manners of the English aristocracy." How far contemporary journalism has moved from these halcyon days.

Today, not even news of international importance has always been reported. For example, the dictatorial behavior and the background of the overthrow of the Romanian dictator, Ceausescu, were never recorded. He had instructed the Patriarchs of the Romanian churches to get their rural priests to recruit tens of thousands of peasant families to provide young offspring as national wards of adoption. These small children were sent to military barracks and were housed in tiny cribs, without loving care. The purpose? To create "the new Soviet man." Such craziness was little reported until unsuspecting American couples began adopting these brain-damaged children, sometimes under the auspices of World Vision.[12]

Nor was it recorded that Petru Dugulescu, a Baptist pastor in Timosoara, a small town on the Romanian border with Hungry, initiated the revolution on New Year's Eve 1989. As his congregation emerged from the evening service, he commanded them to kneel every thousand yards and say the Lord's Prayer while marching from the suburb into the main square. By this time, the crowd had grown to over forty thousand people, all kneeling and chanting the Lord's Prayer. City after city followed in sync through the following three days, until the revolution reached the capital, Bucharest. The Western world was never informed. The Romanian Revolution had all been brought about by peaceful congregants reciting the Lord's Prayer!

Another aspect of press betrayal is to recount, years later, a story that was false from the beginning. One can now even watch the story, on YouTube, concerning the

---

12. James M. Houston, *Memoirs of a Joyous Exile and a Worldly Christian* (Eugene, OR: Wipf & Stock, 2019).

National Prayer Breakfast in Washington, DC. More than a decade ago a young journalist joined a small weekly Prayer Breakfast led by the two young sons of Doug Coe, one of its leaders. The journalist pretended that he was a "religious seeker" as a cover to then report his biased findings to the national press. The national newspaper that had hired him thus condones personal treachery as "press business." They then raked up the story recently to further destroy the reputation of the national movement, as if it was a disclosure from a "mafia" family.

In fact, the National Prayer Breakfast movement originated after General Eisenhower was inaugurated as President in 1953. As Supreme Commander of Allied forces in the European theatre, "Ike" had relied on prayer and Bible reading as he made momentous decisions. Later, when elected President, one of his early acts was to proclaim Saturday, July 4, 1953, a National Day of Prayer, just as November 11 at 11:00 a.m., Armistice Day, is still observed internationally for the troops fallen in the two world wars.[13] But has the national press ever bothered to find out the actual origin

---

13. In 1958 Eisenhower moved the date of the National Day of Prayer to the first day of October 1958. The National Prayer Breakfast is generally held on the first Thursday of February (in Eisenhower's presidency it was called the Presidential Prayer Breakfast, with the name change in 1970).

of the National Prayer Breakfast? Clearly, the press reporter and his seniors who have recently ridiculed the National Prayer Breakfast, as if it was an apparatus of a "Mafia" family, have no idea of this historical heritage. Yet they continue to publish this defamation of the truth.

Conclusion

Despite the technical brilliance of space travel, with its visions of human colonies in outer space, and the robotics of artificial intelligence, we are now entering a new dark age. Lewis foresaw, and Malik shouted against, the fundamental presuppositions of the humanities that are characterized by many absolutes or "-isms": naturalism; subjectivism; rationalism; skepticism; idealism; materialism; "technologism." They all degenerate into relativism and cynicism, and end up in nihilism. Should hard-working parents, wanting their children to have "a better education than they had," invest hard-earned savings on such investment for their children's future?

As Kierkegaard saw all too clearly, as did Rembrandt and Simmel, our deepening of soul desire is either directed toward God or toward the demonic. These prophets saw that the entranceway into the demonic is erotica. But primordial to this lies the revolt in the Garden of Eden: "Has God said?" It all pivots on the uniting theme in this small book, that the erosion of basic trust leads to a life of treachery and betrayal.

10

Challenging a "Fluid Culture"

Modern physics is based upon "solid" and "fluid" physics, whereas human culture has depended on being "solid" to promote a lasting civilization. But as the Polish sociologist Zygmunt Bauman (1925-2017) has demonstrated, postmodern culture has become destabilized as a "fluid culture." It is the end result of the grand betrayal of Western civilization. It is analogous to the fall of the Roman Empire, when the Germanic tribes burst through its Roman frontier and destroyed its civilization. However, what Bauman does not analyze is "the death of the past."

What the Oxford historian J. H. Plumb deplored in his book *The Death of the Past* was the loss of interest in history, both in "Oxbridge" and in society at large. Then the dictum comes into play, as it was written concerning the fall of the Roman Empire: "He who forgets the lessons of the past, is bound to repeat their mistakes."

Plumb was writing to a postwar generation who were calling themselves "postmodern." How can anything be "postmodern" unless it is futuristic? No, it was not about temporal categories of what is past or present, but as a term that was beginning to be used in architecture. "Postmodern" is when architects create a collage of historical styles of buildings and blend them into one construction: not Romanesque, gothic, or baroque but a mixture of them and others too. Such "fluidity" of style was the opening omen of the oncoming fluidity of mind, and then of culture, that Bauman was to identify as a new mindset. But Bauman, unlike Simmel, was only a sociologist, not a philosopher of culture. Likewise, J. H. Plumb was a modern historian who betrayed Christian historiography.

Another betrayer is the French existential historiographer Michel de Certau (1925-1986). Certau's *The Writing of History* is really providing a post-Freudian perspective on history as a literary flow in "writing history" from authorial intent. Certau's "history" evaporates, as did Freud's *Moses and Monotheism*. Both authors contributed to the making of the fluid culture in which we are now immersed.[1]

In order to find direction, we have to turn to the Christian historiographer Jean Daniélou, who proclaims Christ as "The Lord of History."[2] As the epistle

---

1. Michel de Certau, *The Writing of History*, trans. Tom Conley (New York: Columbia University Press, 1988).
2. Jean Daniélou, S.J., *The Lord of History: Reflections on the Inner Meanings of History*, trans. Nigel Abercrombie (1958; repr.,

to the Hebrews states: Christ entered "once" into that holy place, as a unique, irrevocable event in human history, never to be repeated. Hence Christian history is progressive, not cyclical as pagan/secular history is. Nor is it like Greek perfectionism, always being the same. Rather as Augustine's *City of God* demonstrated, all the great creative decisions of God which have determined the course of history, such as the creation of the world, of mankind, the covenant with Abraham, and the resurrection and life eternal determine the destiny of mankind. Ever since, Christian historiography has been a depiction of the faithfulness of God, who keeps covenant with all generations of his faithful followers. It is an economy of progress.

Another Christian historian, Herbert Butterfield, critiques "academic history" as being self-sufficient.[3] For history must have an interpretation. Differing notions of history can have dangerous consequences, for history is not like an empirical science. Nor is it a Marxist view of history, as depicting only the social consequences of certain aspects of the past. Unabashedly, Sir Herbert is claiming that the Christian historian is part historian and part theologian. Yet there can be bogus Christian as well as secular historians. What counts in

---

Cleveland: Meridian, 1968).

3. Herbert Butterfield, *Christianity and History* (London: Collins, 1949).

the end is the quality of life produced by our research and teaching. As I tell my students, if at the end of a lecture I have not given the audience the experience of joy, I have failed to provide Christian communication.

The Fluidity of Religion

But the fluidity of culture has gone beyond what Bauman, and indeed what most Christians, could ever imagine—the fluidity of religion. A new book, *When One Religion Isn't Enough: The Lives of Spiritually Fluid People*,[4] now advocates this "new fluidity." The author, Duane Bidwell, is an ordained Presbyterian minister and professor of practical theology, spiritual care, and counseling at Claremont School of Theology in California. His book is endorsed by a scholar such as Paul F. Knitter, who has published *Without Buddha I Could Not Be a Christian*.

What is the core of such travesty of truth? It is for the search for union and unity of things per se. Like deism, it is an abstraction of human thought. Then it is processed by religiosity, again an abstraction, as the experience of being shaped by a religious multiplicity of community bonds, as if a child was not nurtured by one set of parents but requires a mosaic of ethnic religious traditions: Buddhist, Christian, Hindu, Is-

---

4. Duane R. Bidwell, *When One Religion Isn't Enough: The Lives of Spiritually Fluid People* (Boston: Beacon, 2018).

lamic, pagan—you name them. Of course, add the new movability of globalization, with its accompanying refugees, mixed religious marriages, and the like, and then multiple religious bonds result. Who then is the author accountable to for this mish-mash? Well, of course, to readers who want this confusion of mixed feelings, emotions, and mindsets. One is then also accountable to all the eclectic readers of books purveyed in New Age bookstores under the category of "religious spirituality."

In all this potpourri, the writer is defensive about being spiritually fluid. For such writers do not seriously study other religions nor evaluate them. They pulse with contradictions, so like a new Martin Luther, Duane Bidwell states: [T]his is where I stand. I am Buddhist and Christian. Jesus is my savior, and Buddha is my teacher. Jesus restores me over and over again. He gives me life. He heals (although not usually all at once) and sometimes that healing can be painful."[5] So much blasphemy follows that I dare not repeat it all. But what is clear that for him, religion and spirituality are the same. He is not monistic, like even Muslims are, but pluralistic. So there is not one mountain like Sinai, but many mountains. "Each religious and spiritual path leads to its own mountain." Each is unique.

5. Bidwell, *When One Religion Isn't Enough*, 3.

Then why does Bidwell write such nonsense? He states, "This book attempts in a small way the mending of creation."[6] Yet he denies it to be a "cafeteria religion." It is, he claims, a new kind of scholarship that weaves thought with compassion. He wants to be integrative for people who are restless in heart. But his appeal is seductive. He confesses:

> I think of such people, myself included, as spiritually fluid. Their religious beliefs and behaviors flow among the traditions for a day or a season to fit the landscape of their lives. Like a river that incorporates various streams and tributaries—a thundering cataract in one place and quiet wetland in another—their spirits adapt to or incorporate multiple experiences, communities, spiritual catalysts, that nourish and mold who they are at a given moment.[7]

It is all beautifully metaphorical and sermonic. But is not all this like "the hiss of the cobra" in the Garden of Eden? It promises wisdom, compassion, life-changing experiences, the cure of souls, reconciliation, peace-loving communities, and all the promises of the Christian Gospel.[8] But it is the message of the false prophets in the Old Testament and of the false teachers given us

---

6. Bidwell, *When One Religion Isn't Enough*, 8.
7. Bidwell, *When One Religion Isn't Enough*, 16.
8. Bidwell, *When One Religion Isn't Enough*, 150-51.

in the New Testament. What we are now witnessing is a liquidity of culture far deeper than even Zygmunt Bauman foresaw fifty years ago.

The Fluidity of Sexuality

Both in the churches as well as in society at large, a new fluidity of sexual "mores" is taking place. Those pastors advocating gay marriage can solemnly do so in terms of "husband" and "wife" yet dismiss sexual difference at the same time. Indeed, homosexuality is accepted as "caring" and being pastorally "acceptable" or even "sensitive" by organized churches. Schools are instructing children to "choose your own sexual preference" as if a small child has the developed consciousness to make such a choice. Gay parades have become civic events. With deep sadness, I am compelled to ask, What about biology? For even the flowers, the insects, and the animals are all created to be sexually distinguished.

Abortion is another issue, especially when a teenager learns from a mother, "I tried to abort you when you were a fetus." Divorce has escalated, and childhood wounds are exacerbated in adulthood; one wounded partner wounding the other with their childhood inheritance. As Christians, we need to proclaim that sexuality throws no light upon love, but only through love can we learn to understand sexuality. It is because we live in a loveless culture that our society has become so confused about sex.

Betrayal of Teenagers Today

As "the sins of the fathers are passed on to the children," so too the negative inheritances of previous cultures are now intensifying the wounded emotions of our youth today. In self-protection, they have become desensitized, "strangers to their own emotions." How often their lament is, "I don't know how I feel," although they do know they are hurting and hurting others too: parents against children and children against parents, siblings against siblings.

It is as if, instead of the home being a safe haven from the outside world, civil war has started within, and has expanded to create an emotionally cancerous condition throughout the whole society. A cancer induced by personal stress has become the cancer of the body politic. We are experiencing a pandemic of emotional distrust, starting with children distrusting parents, and parents distrusting children, and all distrusting the society around them.

What Malcolm Muggeridge scornfully called "musak" and "newsak" surrounds us in the elevator taking us up to the condos of our high rise buildings, "the monumental cathedrals" of postmodern life, where we dwell alienated and alone. It is all the end of "a long betrayal" unless there rise up some brave witnesses of the love of God who proclaim that there is another story of trust.

Another Story: Of Trust

But there have always been God's faithful servants who have stood valiantly for the reality of truth, historically grounded in the past deeds of God's loyalty. Such were the early Christians, who were martyred in the first century. Then there were those who confronted the cultural challenge, at the fall of the Roman Empire, notably Benedict of Nursia (c. 480-547). Benedict composed a monastic rule that would shape the next centuries. I believe it can do so again in our next millennium. It was both strict and yet moderate as a live-able rule.

Based on *stabilitas loci*, or the vow of constancy, the monks stayed for life in one community. They shared their possessions and committed to chastity, daily silence, prayer, and humility. As the Benedictine movement spread into Western Europe, it stabilized the Charlemagne Empire, becoming a Christian replica of the pagan Roman Empire. This new empire blossomed through the tenth and eleventh centuries when it needed the reform of the monastic revival, promoted by the Cistercians in the eleventh and twelfth centuries and again by the Jesuits in the sixteenth century.

The revival today of *stabilitas loci* offers encouraging signs of hope in the face of "cultural fluidity." But we need new congregations that are biblically based, with consistent Christian discipleship and accountability in daily confession and repentance, to sustain the extraordinary lifestyle of what it has meant to be called and to be recognized as "Christian."

Who Is a Christian?

We conclude then with the perennial question: "Who is a Christian?"[9] We ask it in spite of the plethora of Christian art, Christian education, Christian ministry, Christian publishing, and all the busyness of our lives today.

Following World War II, a new monastic order was founded by Hans Urs von Balthasar (1905-1988) and his friend, Adrienne von Speyr (1902-1967). They named it the Order of St. John. At great personal sacrifice, Von Balthasar left the Jesuit Order to cofound this new order and to prepare for the conciliar reform of the Second Vatican Council. Yet for years Von Balthasar went unrecognized, a penalty for leaving the Jesuit order, and receiving the Cardinal's hat just three days before he died!

---

9. See James M. Houston and Jens Zimmerman, *Sources of Christian Self: A Cultural History of Christian Identity* (Grand Rapids: Eerdmans, 2018).

Unique in the history of Catholic canon law, the Vatican is now in process of the canonization of both founders, male and female together as saints of the Church. So extensive are the works of Von Balthasar, in patristic studies and in the biographies of the early fathers, in theology and apologetics, that he left us a summary of his works titled *My Work in Retrospect*.[10] Yet modestly he chose to bow in deference to his coworker, Adrienne von Speyr, who devoted multiple volumes to her meditations on the Gospel of John. Meditatively, Von Spehr affirms: "As the beginning, God declares *that* he is. As the Word, he declares *who* he is. If God were known only as the beginning, the world would not know who he is. The beginning is the God to whom there is no access. He is the incommensurable—so far above us that we are not merely unable to conceive it, but also remain unmoved by its greatness."[11]

She then proceeds:

> And just as Jesus Christ, the Word made flesh, is in every word of creation and of the order of salvation, being the very foundation and aim of everything unexpressed and hidden, so, too, are the Church and the sacraments. They, too, are

---

10. Hans Urs von Balthasar, *My Work in Retrospect* (San Francisco: Ignatius, 1993)

11. Adrienne von Speyr, *The Word: A Meditation on John's Gospel* (San Francisco: Ignatius, 1994), 10-11.

present in the Unexpressed Word of God, contained in the Word from the beginning, because while not yet instituted and still unexpressed, formless, and to us, unimaginable, they are already contained and themselves contain that which constitutes the fullness of the love of God. Both the sacraments and the Church were in the beginning, as they now exist, as his love, foreseen in every detail. They are, therefore, unexpressed but most really present in the opening verses of John's Prologue.[12]

She concludes her meditation:

But the Son can be known because he was in the Word, and because we have acknowledged his Incarnation. He forms the bridge between seeing our neighbor, a duty incumbent upon us, and seeing God, which is impossible. And then again the apostle John forms the bridge between us and the Son, through his entirely human, friendly love for the Lord. One should not scorn genuine human friendship as a way to God and certainly not set up an antithesis between the love of one's friends and the love of one's neighbor. For since we are human, living in a human framework, Christian love itself unfolds gradually, starting from friendship.[13]

---

12. Von Speyr, *The Word*, 12-13.
13. Von Speyr, *The Word*, 159.

No wonder even the sophisticated communicator and national poet laureate T. S. Eliot wrote on the cover of her book: "Von Speyr's book does not lend itself to any classification that I can think of. It is not dogmatic theology; still less is it exegesis . . . there is nothing to do but to submit oneself to it; if the reader emerges without having been crushed by it, he will find himself strengthened and exhilarated by a new experience of Christian sensibility."

Today, we are living in a finite world. We are what C. S. Lewis called "men without chests," for only finite things mean anything to us. The infinite is what we cannot imagine, and that is why it means nothing to us. It has none of the characteristics we know. It cannot be felt, it cannot be measured, and, being incomprehensible, it does not awaken any demands in us. Contrastively, Lewis speaks of the transposition given to the Christian as "the weight of glory," for as the Christian faith teaches us, it turns our original desires and wants to reveal what is still hidden within us: our deepest spiritual longings.[14]

The experience of this, for the Christian, intensifies the sheer frustration that we feel today in trying to convey and to convince non-Christians of what God is like, who he is, and to narrate the gospel as Rem-

---

14. C. S. Lewis, *The Weight of Glory* (New York: Harper Collins, 2001), 39.

brandt did so brilliantly in art. It is what the apostle Paul described as "walking in darkness" like prisoners in a dungeon.

What then breaks the barrier of the incommunicable to the secularist today? It is God's spoken word, the biblical Scriptures, by the Holy Spirit that penetrates into the dark prison of secularism with the light of divine revelation.

But unlike the models of human thought that we have depicted, such models are inadequate for portraying the mystery of Christians becoming the children of God. So in addition to von Speyr's model, there is also the Reformed Protestant model with its focus upon the sacrament of baptism and new birth.

Facing Our Mortality

As medical science blesses us with advanced age, and as the distance increases between the death of loved ones and our own death, we need to apply this to unite our temporal presence with the eternal presence of our loved ones who have died. Those who have died, have now celebrated their "graduation" on earth and heard these words acclaimed: "Well done thou good and faithful servant, enter now into the joy of your Lord!" Our "graduation" is still to be fulfilled. But now, only a thin veil separates their presence eternally with the Lord and our temporal presence with the Lord. Their death only binds us closer together with our Lord so that "practicing the presence of the Lord," as Brother Lawrence exemplified, becomes sweeter and dearer as time passes.

Therefore, let us not succumb to the subtle betrayal of our deceased loved ones, not just of their memory which has become dulled, but of their continual presence that should be always be still present to us. Rather we are more enriched by bereavement in an exchange for the mutuality of divine presence they share with us, dead and alive. Then like the apostle Paul, we can rejoice that "We are more than conquerors [over death] through Him who loved us through death into resurrection from the dead." As Rosenstock-Huessy has wisely said: "The most important fact is that we know of, every individual's physical death, is not a fact of past or of present, but of the future . . . the word "future" attains its full meaning only when we assume and recognize the possibility of death between now and then."[15]

---

15. Eugen Rosenstock-Huessy, *Lifelines: Quotations from His Works*, ed. Clinton C. Carver (Norwich, VT: Argo, 1988), 13.

11

Christian Faithfulness to the Gospel of Christ

Outstanding among God's faithful people have been the Mennonites. Named after the reformer Menno Simons (1496-1561), a Friesen priest who called for a radical reform and rebaptism beginning around 1536.[1] Persecuted through the following centuries, often by fellow Christians, Mennonites later migrated to the United States and Canada in the eighteenth, nineteenth, and early twentieth century as well as to South America in the later part. But the largest migration was to the Ukraine from Prussia in the early nineteenth century and then to Russia after 1870. They prospered in the black, fertile soils of Russia until Lenin then ordered collectivization under Marxist theory. The following personal letters from Ukraine to relatives in Canada summarize what tragically followed.[2]

---

1. The Anabaptist movement had earlier roots in the radical wing of the Reformation beginning in Switzerland and its environs in the 1520s.
2. Unpublished Wiebe family correspondence, translated by Agatha Klassen and Agnes Klassen (Abbotsford, BC, 2010).

Aug. 28. From Orenburg, Russia, sometime after 1928-29 and forced collectivization.

From your uncle Paul Wiebe

Here in Russia farming is different from what it used to be. All the farms are Collective Farms, two to three villages farming together . . . bread is rationed, but there is never enough . . . we live, very meagerly . . . there is no sugar available. But I don't want to complain. You can read through the lines how things are going on . . . I did not write this letter by myself as my eye-sight is very poor, clinically blind, so I ask someone to write for me. Be so kind as to greet all my friends from me, also the Bergen's children. It will give me great joy if you could do this for me because I am old and alone. Hearty greetings to everyone from your uncle Paul Wiebe.

March 16, 1928

Dear Auntie, cousins and children! . . . I wish for all of you the best of health in body and soul. Thank God we too are well! We received your valued letter . . . and many people came from the village to see the card you had sent and read the letter. We had a good crop this year, but all of it has been sent away, even the small amounts which people had saved from past years and stored in the attics is all gone. The floors were swept clean. In places where the crops were small, people are already finding themselves without sufficient bread. There is nowhere to buy or borrow, and the next harvest is far away. We are in a sad time again . . . the Preachers of the Word have had a hard time. But we are glad we know who is at the helm and has everything in His hands. He guides the hearts and minds of people like streams of water. I have sometimes said we are experiencing these things because the Lord wants to prepare us so that we are ready when He thinks fit to open the door for us so that we can emigrate. May God give us much strength to be prepared to do His will . . . That the Lord is coming soon, we know well.

Feb. 5, 1933

[To post this] we have to walk 16 miles [across the snow], but love drives us.

How things will turn out this year we don't know. Sometimes such a longing for our heavenly home comes over me. Someday we will meet with our loved ones at the Throne of God. Oh that no one is missing. Our brother still is in exile, but we know nothing about him . . . That is very hard for our dear father. We trust everything to God who has never made a mistake . . . The future lies before us very darkly but God has never forsaken us and will continue to uphold us even in dark times. Unless you have experienced it, you do not know how difficult it is to trust in God when your cupboards are bare, and there is no one to fill them. "Trust and obey, for there is no other way to be happy in Jesus but to trust and obey." Even if the Lord leads us in difficult ways, our prayer is that we remain faithful to the end. He will refine us and purify us and help us get rid of all which is unfit for the Kingdom of God. By helping us you are workmen in God's hand. Jesus says: "Before you call in the midst of pain and strife, help me to be quiet and patient. I will answer you."

Sunday, September 11, 1933. In the midst of the Stalin-made famine, the Holodomor.

We thank God we are well in body and spirit. Today I come as a visitor with a heavy heart . . . Peter was ordered to present himself and so they arrested him at once. He was not able to return home and remains imprisoned in Orloff. We are harassed without cause—where are we to find the nearly 1000 pud they are demanding—harvests are very poor and yet we are required to provide so much grain. That is why he is being punished—a five year sentence . . . Thursday they came for our chickens, today they took our cow—soon they will sell everything we have and then what will become of us? Only a loving God knows how we feel and how much more we can bear. Please pray for us.

December 19, 1957

"I am the Lord who heals you" (Exodus 15:26). Yes, my Lord and healer of the soul. Bless me and most beloved and faithful cousin and family! Merry Christmas and a happy New Year and good health in your daily life. I received your precious letter last week, many thanks . . . I would like to give you a little glimpse of what everyone is doing . . .

I got married in 1928 when I was 38 years old. My husband was a widower. He had four children of his own and three foster children who belonged to his brother. Both parents had died. He has 3 sons and one daughter, all of them baptized in the river. My husband was a Christian too, and I was saved when I was 15 years old. Our girls are saved and baptized, and our three sons are married. They don't live very far away from us. But now one son is living in Germany . . . During all these difficult years, the Lord did not forsake us . . . I am already 68 years old.[3]

The Persecuted Christians of Contemporary China

During the 1980s, I had the privilege of meeting at night several Chinese pastors. Such was Brother Sam

---

3. Unpublished Wiebe family correspondence.

in south China who was condemned to ten years hard labor uncoupling the coal wagons in the coalmines. It is dangerous work; his predecessor had been killed doing this task. Eventually released, he was protected by a Bible given to him by Billy Graham and signed by President Reagan, himself a devout Christian.

Another Chinese leader I met in the same locality had spent some eight years cleaning out the city's municipal's sewage system, waist high in the sewage with its noxious odor. He recalled how he would sing at his task: "I dwell in the garden alone, but He walks with me, and He talks with me." He could smell the sweet odor of His presence, as the composer of the Song of Songs had done millennia ago.

Today I am in constant correspondence with a Christian publisher in China who left his position in a prestigious publishing company to pastor a house-church and then spent many years under house arrest. Yet with his indomitable spirit of loyalty to Christ, he is still translating and publishing Christian books from the West to nourish the souls and minds of fellow Christians!

Queen Wilhemina of the Netherlands

Living in a completely different world, Queen Wilhelmina (1880-1962) wrote a book titled *Lonely, but*

Not Alone.[4] Abraham Vareide, who founded The International Council for Christian Leadership, did a summary of her book:

> Throughout the world, there is an immense emptiness, a conscious or unconscious longing, which can be met and fulfilled in Christ. There is a longing for brotherhood, which can be realized through a living, dynamic union with Him and his guidance. Thus we become less deterred by the intellectualism, materialism, and fatalism of our time.
>
> The Hidden fellowship with Christ has become increasingly meaningful to me. After fifty years in the pulsating life as Queen of the Netherlands, this is now a great reality, nurtured in solitude and meditation on Jesus' words. It is God the Father who has revealed His glory in Jesus as man, and Who in him took upon Himself our guilt on the cross, and in his resurrection and complete redemption has restored the broken relationship. Christ is the fulfillment of that which other religions have tried to find. He is the supreme answer to the deepest question. Where the human mind must stop, God comes in Christ with the divine answer to the quest of His creatures. He has kindled in me the burning desire to relieve human suffering and to meet

---

4. Wilhelmina Princess of the Netherlands, *Lonely but Not Alone*, trans. John Peereboom (London: Hutchinson, 1960).

the need of my fellowmen everywhere. Christ has lifted me and permitted me to see the reality of God. He has permitted me to see that man, in spite of his brutality, as revealed during the past world wars and the world over, may become a child of God through the redeeming power of Jesus Christ, who by His love restores the most fallen, being fully into his birthright with God. Wherever you are, and wherever you look, you live and breathe in a universe which is guided by wisdom and patience, the source of which is love. Everywhere you meet the bright reflection of His person. Could anything but inexpressible joy take possession of you then? The Almighty Creator's redemption fills you with jubilation.

It is Christ's message which we must bring forward to all mankind. This is the secret of our spiritual power, which we must show forth in our deeds, , in the little things as in the great. Are we willing to receive this salvation which Christ offers us, and to listen to God's fatherly will? Are we willing to join with Him in the Spirit of Christ to work for the solution of the problems around us? Would you join hands with Him and with others to remove misunderstandings, poverty, and discrimination, and seek to replace insecurity and hopelessness with hope and a positive faith, until He shall be all in all?

These things have come to me as a matter of divine revelation. My life has been led and has found its meaning in the higher plan of Jesus

Christ. It is my prayer that His joy may come to all men everywhere, and that all human joy may find its fulfillment in Him. He stands at the door and knocks; if any man will hear His voice and open the door, He will come in to him to sup with him.[5]

What the Western world of the press never knew nor was ever reported was that Queen Wilhelmina had, in God's providence, appointed Ernst van Eeghen as her Honorary President of the Veterans Association of the Netherlands after the War and before her death. Van Eeghen, along with three Christian Soviet leaders, who also were veterans, and three Christian American leaders, saved the world from a nuclear holocaust.[6]

As I began this reflective study I spoke of my need of forgiveness on a daily basis when I do not speak out against the public ridicule of Christianity. Yes, like Peter we have often denied our Lord, but like Peter we can say as a Christian, "If you are insulted because of the name of Christ . . . you are blessed, for the Spirit of glory and of God rests on you" (1 Pet. 4:16). Thus, this book is intended as a "wake-up call" for our generation.

---

5. Abraham Vereide,

6. See James M. Houston, *Memoirs of a Joyous Exile and a Worldly Christian* (Eugene, OR: Wipf & Stock, 2019), 97-108. See also Giles Scott-Smith, "A Dutch Dartmouth: Ernst van Eeghen's Private Campaign to Defuse the Euromissiles Crisis," *New Global Studies* 8, no. 1 (2014): 141-52.

The Grand Betrayal of Western Christianity

We Christians should be passionate against secularism as the grand betrayal of Western civilization and, therefore, of Christianity.

APPENDIX

Responding to Being a Christian

As you put this book down, your reaction may well be: "It's all very well for a scholarly response to the contemporary indifference to Christianity. But how do I respond to daily conversations with unbelievers?" This appendix may help you.

Hell

Especially in the Bible belt culture, droves of young people are abandoning their parents' faith because what they heard as teenagers was: "If you don't believe in God, you're going to hell."

In any discussion, ask: What is meant by "hell"? In Dante's *Inferno*, Satan is frozen and immobilized totally in the depth of a frozen lake. Dante is suggesting "hell" is the incapacity to receive or give love.

Spiritual, Not Religious

As a Christian, I'm not "religious" either. The only way of release from bondage to many things such as money, sex, or drink, is by becoming a Christian! So both of

Secularism

The definition of secularism is "the Negation of Worship." But how can you possibly be a non-worshipper when everyday, as we have just seen, we are all worshipping something, especially money? Animals are instinctual beings while humans are relational beings, so only humans are worshippers.

Atheism

Atheists have really thought things through, or their parents did before them. Perhaps they or their parents became convinced Marxists, believing with Karl Marx that "religion is the opiate of the masses."

The problem they face however is that because we are "humans", we are all worshippers. You cannot live in a relational void of "nihilism." You must trust your friends and family at some level. Otherwise you are already alone in a tomb of the self. Even hermits in the Amazonian forests or steppes of Asia have connections with the outside world.

Loneliness

"So I would just want to ask you, where does love come from? Without love, we can't have friendship." Honest skeptics can only respond, "We don't know."

But Christians do have an answer. For God is love, and he offers us his friendship.

I don't want to spend time arguing and debating. I want to listen to your story, for without it I will never know who you are. I want to learn about your childhood, of the basic trust that was nurtured or betrayed, which has shaped your personality, as it has mine, ever since.

www.ingramcontent.com/pod-product-compliance
Lightning Source LLC
LaVergne TN
LVHW041631070426
835507LV00008B/561